THE TREND OF FISCAL POLICY IN THE UNITED STATES

The Trend of Fiscal Policy in the United States

History of Tax Policy in the 20th Century

By Serge Wilner D'Haiti, CPA

The Trend of Fiscal Policy in the United States
History of Tax Policy in the 20th Century

All rights reserved. No part of this publication may be reproduced, stored in a retrieval system, or transmitted in any form without written permission from the author.

ISBN: 9781731207104
Copyright © 2018 Serge D'Haiti

Cover Design by Jashua Sa-Ra
Edited by Jashua Sa-Ra
Layout by Jashua Sa-Ra

Published by Earthiopia Works 2018

Contents

- 2 - Introduction
- 4 - What is Tax Policy
- 5 - The Theories of Tax Policies
- 7 - Theodore Roosevelt Administration
- 8 - William H. Taft Administration
- 10 - Woodrow Wilson Administration
- 12 - Warren G. Harding Administration
- 13 - John C. Coolidge Administration
- 15 - Herbert Hoover Administration
- 17 - Franklin D. Roosevelt Administration
- 18 - Ronald Reagan Administration
- 20 - Bill Clinton Administration
- 21 - George W. Bush Administration
- 26 - Barack Obama Administration
- 29 - Economy Through the Decades
- 30 - The National Debt
- 37 - Conclusion
- 40 - List of Presidents from 20th-21st Century
- 41 - Treasury Secretaries from 20th-21st Century
- 42 - Bibliography

Dedication

I dedicate this work to all the readers for taking the time out of your busy day to receive the knowledge I have acquired. To Florida Atlantic University, Barry Kaye College of Business, and the professors in my college career who molded my mind to reach my goal as a Certified Public Accountant. Finally, I dedicate this book to all the people who have added to my character. The small talks and heated discussions we had were influences to allow me to perservere in my life. I hope this book gives the motivation and encouragement to continue, excel, and prosper in future endeavors. Ultimately, I want to dedicate this work to the Most High for the vision, strength, and will that is placed inside of me.

Acknowledgement

I would like to give thanks to the Most High for the experience and opportunity of life, the D'Haiti family, the Hester family, and extended members who added pressure to me so that I can shine; the city of West Palm Beach and Palm Beach County School District, Palm Beach Community College, Florida Atlantic University, the gentlemen of Phi Beta Sigma, Inc., the fine ladies of Zeta Phi Beta, Inc., and the "struggle."

THE TREND OF FISCAL POLICY IN THE UNITED STATES

History of Tax Policy in the 20th Century

By Serge Wilner D'Haiti, CPA

Introduction

In every society that is governed by its respective government, there are laws and regulations to maintain order and the continued growth of its society. These laws, regulations, economic growth are the necessary function of the government, for without it, the government would no longer exist, along with its society.

Therefore, the government has to make a compromise with its society so that both entities can grow. The society is complete with individuals, corporations, partnerships, for profit and non-profit organizations, along with alien entities from foreign countries that are located in another country. These entities conduct business, or earn income for the success of themselves, through profit maximization, or providing socially responsible activities that benefit the sectors of society with limited resources.

In addition to these functions in society, the government is established to make the inefficient functions work efficiently. For example, if the for-profits and the non-profits are providing goods and services with limited amount of resources, the government will step in, research the economy or the target market, find the inefficiencies, and apply the appropriate actions that benefit society in a utilitarian approach.

However, these government-provided remedies could have a negative effect and backfire on society, as well as cause more inefficiency instead of resolving the issue.

For example, there was a story about a business owner in the service industry. The owner was in business for more than twenty years. After retiring from the business, the owner decided to donate the business to the country.

Before the donation, three people ran the business for twenty years, which consisted of two managers and one server. The country's government examined the recently donated business. Then an assessment was made and the government asserted that the business was operating inefficiently, so an action was implemented that could allow the government to operate efficiently: adding five servers and other strategies.

The business was widely recognized and never had a problem servicing the public. As soon as the government got a hold of the business, it was not able to survive the future years due to the increase in operating cost.

Therefore, the government's decisions can really affect the lives of the people it serves. However, the government in itself is a business. Ultimately, it must use its authority to remain financially solid. The government implements policy that allows itself to earn income through taxes. Consequently, the government has three ways to increase its revenues: exploit a new tax base, increase the tax rate to its taxpayer, or enlarge an existing tax base.

This research focuses on the trends in tax policies in America in the twentieth century, such George H. W. Bush's "Read My Lips: No New Taxes."

What Is Tax Policy

Tax policy is the government's attitude, objective, and action with respect to its tax system. Tax policy reflects standards that are the most important the policy makers but ultimately their constituents. The government prescribes criteria on the normative standard. The course of action taken into account after the implementation of the policy will yield ideal results. The inefficiencies in the policy are left open for interpretation. These policies are expressed to the public to inform the people how the government will receive support from the taxpayer.

The American Institute of Certified Public Accountant issued an article describing what "Good" tax policies are. In the article, **Guiding Principles of Good Tax Policy** *(2001)*, the AICPA describe that these tax policies that are good for the country as having 10 qualities that will have a positive engagement with individuals and the business community.

Ten Guiding Principles of Good Tax Policy
1. *Equity and Fairness.* Similarly situated taxpayers should be taxed similarly.
2. *Certainty.* The tax rules should clearly specify when the tax is to be paid, how it is to be paid, and how the amount to be paid is to be determined.
3. *Convenience of Payment.* A tax should be due at a time or in a manner that is most likely to be convenient for the taxpayer.
4. *Economy in Collection.* The costs to collect a tax should be kept to a minimum for both the government and taxpayers.
5. *Simplicity.* The tax law should be simple so that taxpayers understand the rules and can comply with them correctly and in a cost-efficient manner.
6. *Neutrality.* The effect of the tax law on a taxpayer's decisions as to how to carry out a particular transaction, or whether to engage in a transaction, should be kept to a minimum.
7. *Economic Growth and Efficiency.* The tax system should not impede or reduce the productive capacity of the economy.
8. *Transparency and Visibility.* Taxpayers should know that a tax exists and how and when it is imposed upon them and others.
9. *Minimum Tax Gap.* A tax should be structured to minimize noncompliance.
10. *Appropriate Government Revenues.* The tax system should enable the government to determine how much tax revenue will likely be collected and when

The Theories of Tax Policies

Supply-Side Economics

The Supply-Side economics is a tax policy theory that provides tax reduction to stimulate the economy. The decrease in the highest tax rates results in ultimately higher generated governmental revenues. The theory is that rate cuts increase the value of income-generated activities from working and investments. Then the people who benefit from the rate cuts and income-activities will simply spend the extra income, which causes an influx of economic growth and job creation.

Classical Standard Economics

The Classical Standard of Economics is that the free market will regulate itself without any intervention from the public sector in the long-run. During this period, economists rejected the idea that government should get involved in private affairs. Their notion was that government should be involved and the businesses have to regulate themselves with the resources available to sustain themselves and their business markets. According to Adam Smith, author of <u>The Wealth of Nations</u>,

> A tax may obstruct the industry of the people and discourage them from applying to certain branches of business, which give maintenance, and employment to great multitudes. While it obligates the people to pay, it may diminish or perhaps destroy some of the funds, which might enable them more easily to do so.

The Classical Standard economist determined price was attributed by the level of output, technology, and wages. These factors will ultimately allows economies to regulate themselves without government intervention and made it unnecessary for the government to get involved in business affairs. This was their attitude back in the 17th and 18th century.

Keynesian Economics

Keynesian economics is a macroeconomic theory based on the idea of 20th century economist John Maynard Keynes. John Keynes proposed that some micro-economic actions have an effect on the macro-economic outcome of an economy to influence output and growth. Keynes argued a solution to a depression was to stimulate the economy with two factors: 1) a reduction in interest rates and 2) increase in expenditures of government investments. Keynes's theory states that investment made by government injects income into the economy and in turn results in more spending in the general economy, which will stimulate more production and investment by the private sector.

The Keynesian theory incorporates saving, consumption, investment, and production level of output and employment in the economy. Theses factors are interrelated with each other, because when employment wages increase, savings made to banks increases along with consumption. As the level of consumption increases, the demand for producing more goods increases, which will require more investment in capital and hiring of more people. Ultimately, the result is more growth in the economy. Moreover, the reverse will occur, which will result in economy decay.

Keynes suggested that governmental policy to be proactive to stimulate the economy in the short run rather than wait for the market to equalize itself in the long run with the laissez faire approach. As Keynes theory suggests, this fiscal policy is only appropriate when unemployment is persistently high and the economy is sluggish to decay stage.

To Keynes, the accelerated factor effect meant:
1) The government and business capabilities complimented each other rather than act as substitutes to the problem of economic downturn;

2) When the government provided stimulus gross domestic product rises and raises the amount of saving, helping to finance the increase in fixed investment;

3) Government investment in public goods that will not be provided by profit-seekers encourage the private sector's growth, and government investment in research, public health, education, and infrastructure will lead to long-term growth potential in gross domestic product.

The United States government formally embraced its fiscal policy responsibilities when Congress enacted the Employment Act of 1946. This legislation charged the Executive Branch with promoting full employment and a stable dollar and resulted in the formation of the President's Council of Economic Advisers. (Jones, 2009)

The Theodore Roosevelt Administration

The War Revenue Reduction Act of 1901

In 1898, progressives came up with the idea of death taxes as a base to raise revenue for the Spanish-American War. Supporters of the tax exclaimed, "The inheritance tax is levied on a class of wealth, a class of property and a class of citizens that do not otherwise pay their fair share of the burden to government." The opponents of the proposal suggested that big businesses would consider liquidating all of their assets in order to eliminate the possibility of accumulating wealth in order to avoid the tax incident, and that would cause those businesses to neglect the capitalism concept: "The growth of capital markets."

The inheritance tax was signed into law 1898 and the rate of tax on the estate was a range of .75% to 15%. The first $10,000 was exempt from the estate tax and bequests to surviving spouse were exempt from estate tax.

The tax was very fair. However, the opponents were thinking that the tax would cause people to avoid the tax altogether, and the government would not raise any revenue. They thought instead, that the economy would deteriorate because big business would abandon the capital markets, which in turn would bring the country's economic growth to a halt.

In the twentieth century, the United States Supreme Court declared the tax constitutional in the Knowlton v. Moore case. Later in 1901, the act was amended to exempt certain gifts to charitable, religious, literary, and educational organizations, and organization that promoted the encouragement of Arts and the prevention of cruelty to children (War Revenue Reduction Act.)

In 1902, the War Revenue Repeal Act was enacted. It was a short-lived act, but in the course of its life, it raised government revenues of $14.1 million dollars.

The William H. Taft Administration

The Payne-Aldrich Tariff Act of 1909

The Payne-Aldrich Tariff Act of 1909 was named after Sereno E. Payne and Nelson W. Aldrich. This bill started in the House of Representatives to lower tariffs on goods being imported in the United States of America. The bill was scheduled to lower 650 tariffs and raise 220 tariffs, while 1,150 were left unchanged. Another provision was added that would have the tariffs studied to identify potential problems or issues that were relevant conflicts, and subsequently propose modification to the tariffs. In addition, the tariffs would have to be well researched before issued into law so that the President and Congress would have access to the information.

The 16th Amendment

William H. Taft supported the 16th amendment as a way to control and regulate big corporations from taking advantage of the tax system without paying their fair share of tax on income. Below is President William H. Taft's message to congress on June 16, 1909:

> "I therefore recommend an amendment to the tariff bill imposing upon ALL CORPORATION AND JOINT STOCK COMPANIES FOR PROFIT, except national banks otherwise taxed, SAVINGS BANKS, and BUILDING AND LOAN ASSOCIATIONS, an excise tax, measured by 2 percent on the net income of such CORPORATIONS. This is an excise tax UPON THE PRIVILEGE of doing business as an ARTIFICIAL ENTITY and of freedom from a general partnership liability enjoyed by those who own the stock. I am informed that 2 per cent of the character would bring into the Treasury of the United States not less than $25,000,000. "The decision of the Supreme Court in the case of SPRECKELS SUGAR REFINING CO. v. MCCLAIN, (192 US 397) seems clearly to establish the principle that such tax as this is an EXCISE TAX upon PRIVILEGE and NOT a direct tax on property, and is within the federal power to tax without apportionment according to population. The tax on net income is preferable to one proportionate to a percentage of the gross receipts, because it is a tax upon success and not failure. It imposes a burden at the source of income at a time when the

CORPORATION is well able to pay and when collection is easy.

"Another merit of this tax is the federal supervision which must be exercised in order to make the law effective over the annual accounts and business transactions OF ALL CORPORATIONS. When the faculty of assuming a corporate form has been of the utmost utility in the business world, it is also true that substantially all of the abuses and all of the evils which have aroused the public to the necessary (sic) of reform were made possible by the use of this very faculty. If now, by a perfectly legitimate and effective system of taxation, we are incidently (sic) able to possess the Government and the stockholders and the public of the knowledge of the real business transactions and the GAINS AND PROFITS OF EVERY CORPORATION IN THE COUNTRY, we have made a long step toward the supervisory CONTROL OF CORPORATIONS which may prevent a further abuse of power.

The Woodrow Wilson Administration

Tariff Reform, Underwood-Simmons Act

President Thomas Wilson expanded opportunities of economics for people at all levels of society for the people at the bottom of society and the people at the top of society. This tariff reform eliminated special programs that gave advantages to the richest and most financially powerful members in society.

Currency Problem and Banking Reform

The Federal Reserve Act of 1913 established 12 regional banks that were operated by the federal government through the Federal Reserve Board, a federal agency appointed by the President.

The Federal Reserve Board could adjust interest rates and the nation's money supply. The Federal Reserve Banks authorized the issue of currency based on government securities and commercial paper, which are loans made by banks to businesses. This was used as tool to control the circulation of money and ultimately the economy.

The Federal Reserve Board was empowered to make adjustments to the interest rate, which indirectly controlled the rate of interest the banks charge to other banks and public through the discount rate. In addition, the Federal Reserve Board also set requirement to member banks on the amount of funds to have on reserve from the deposits credited to the balance sheet. This act was Thomas Woodrow Wilson most important domestic achievement and successor administrators currently use to date.

Clayton Antitrust Act of 1914

The Clayton Act was similar to the Sherman Antitrust act, however, it protected laborers, farmers, and like organizations from monopolization through unfair practices. The Clayton act prohibited price-fixing and kept directors from serving on one company's board and serving on competing board of companies in the same or one industry. It also gave the Federal Trade Commission authority to investigate and scrutinize businesses for corrupt, unfair, and anti-competitive business practices.
The Wilson Administration abolished child labor and required 8 hour work days for railroad work after going on strike. Finally, President Wilson levied

a new income tax system, which financed half of the $33 billion to enter World War I while the other cost was financed with Liberty Bonds.

The Harding Administration

President Warren G. Harding had a very interesting administration. It has been called "the most criminal atmosphere in the White House history." Some cabinet members were receiving bribes and kickbacks. Others cabinet members committed pilferage with oil reserves in the United States. Moreover, others cabinet members were supporting the black markets with alcohol and narcotics.

Budget and Accounting Act of 1921

Budget and Accounting Act gave the President an uniformed budget, rather than receiving an individual budget from each cabinet member's secretary to submit to Congress. The General Accounting Office was formed to audit government expenditures.
Andrew Mellon, the Treasury Secretary, was allowed to push through the most substantial tax cuts for wealthy citizens and large corporations. This allowed individuals earning $1 million a year to pay one third of their income tax compared to the income tax paid by the same individual with the same income in the year 1920.

Fordney-McCumber Tariff Act of 1922

The Fordney-McCumber Act implementation reversed the downward movements in interest rates during the Wilson Administration. In addition, the Harding Administration did the complete opposite from William Taft, who had worked vigorously to regulate big business, by regulating monopolization and discouraged anti-competitiveness in business. The Harding Administration encouraged the Federal Trade Commission, the Interstate Commerce Commission, and the Justice Department to cooperate with the corporations in their criminal activities, corruption, and conspiracies.

Revenue Act of 1921

The Revenue Act of 1921 provided tax relief to taxpayers after the tax increase from the Wilson Administration. Warren G. Harding and Andrew Mellon provided tax relief to all taxpayers after World War I; however again, the richest citizens bore less of the tax burden.

The Coolidge Administration

After President Harding's death in 1923, his Vice President, Calvin Coolidge, completed his term in 1924. However, the public was very skeptical of electing him as the next President because of the incitements that occurred during his predecessor's administration.

The Revenue Act of 1924

The Revenue Act of 1924, or also known as the Mellon Bill, cut federal income tax rates and established the United States Tax Court under the name Board of Tax Appeals.

The Mellon bill provided tax rebates to individuals for 1924 and the overall corporate tax burden was lowered after the bill increased the surtax exemption and repeal of the war-excess profits and capital stock taxes. The government tax revenues decreased from $4 billion to $1.7 billion according to Louis Alan Talley, Tax Specialist. At the time, the country had recently come out of a war under the Wilson Administration. In addition, due to Wilson's unsupportive attitude towards the wealthy class and big business' operation, higher taxes were charged on the individuals who had the resources to evade fair taxation through tax shelters at their convenience and at their luxury. The income tax rates were raised to generate revenue and minimize tax avoidance. The Wilson administration charged higher taxes to the top earners in the country.

After World War I issues were resolved, especially since the United States tried to avoid entering into the war in the first place, the Coolidge administration found it necessary to cut the taxes to allow the American people to have relief from paying high taxes. However, the opponents of the Mellon Bill did not want to allow the evil seeds of the individual to be able to take advantage of the tax system. For that reason, the public wanted a full disclosure of the taxes paid to be itemized. The Coolidge Administration put up great resistance to prohibit the full disclosure provision.

Public Disclosure in the 1920s

"The Revenue Act of June 2, 1924 made public disclosure the rule for both individual and corporate taxpayers. Advocates of disclosure argued that publicity would discourage evasion and improper business conduct. Robert Howell, Republican senator from Nebraska, argued that "secrecy is of the greatest aid to corruption" and contended, "[T]oday the price of liberty is not only eternal vigilance [sic] but also publicity" (quoted in Leff, (1984), p. 67). That statute made public not the tax returns themselves, but rather the names and addresses of individuals and corporations filing returns along with their respective tax payments. (10) Before the 1924 elections, newspapers across the country published the names and tax payments of large companies, celebrities, and local residents. The New York Times filled pages with lists showing the amounts of tax paid by thousands of people, and ran stories listing the names of prominent New Yorkers who had paid no income tax.

President Coolidge and his Treasury secretary, Andrew Mellon, vigorously opposed making tax return information public. They and other opponents of publicity argued that disclosure gave hucksters access to names of wealthy taxpayers to target for scams, compromised business secrecy, and proved useless, and perhaps harmful, to tax administration and collection efforts. With the passage of the Act of Feb. 26, 1926, the law was changed so that only the names and addresses of taxpayers, and not their tax liabilities, were public. (11)" (Lenter, Slemrod, Shackelfor, 2003)

The Hoover Administration

Herbert Hoover, our thirty-first President, from 1929-1933 made some tough decisions that affected the heart and bloodline of America, because of the great depression of 1929 and the Wall Street Crash of 1929. He was slow to provide relief on the federal level to families who were suffering from high unemployment in the economy (Herbert Hoover 2009). Some writings say that President Hoover was hesitant to provide federal relief to farmers and refused to utilize the human capital in the urban areas, which could have mitigated the unemployment rate. For example, "Hoover vetoed a bill that would have created a federal unemployment agency and also opposed a plan to create a public works programme." (Hoover 2009)

The unemployment rate made it difficult for everyone. During this time, the First World War veterans discovered that the number of jobs were scarce, when the veterans, too, were unemployed during those rough times. In May 1932, these ex-soldiers marched to Washington to demand a bonus be paid immediately instead of installments paid over twenty years.
Near to the end of the Herbert Hoover Administration, the Revenue Act of 1932 was passed. This was the first time in American history that a piece of legislation was passed to increase peacetime tax revenues. He had a classical view on the economy. The people at that time called his strategy a "counter cyclical fiscal policy."

Herbert Hoover believed that tax cuts would boost business confidence, and he wanted to change the lives of all Americans through regulations and encouraging volunteerism. He closed tax loopholes for the wealthy. He believed private and public cooperation was the way to long-term growth of the country he served. Hoover feared that too much government intervention would destroy individualism and cause Americans to rely on government assistance, rather than Americans being self-reliant.

The Smoot-Hawley Tariff Act of 1931

The Smoot-Hawley Tariff Act of 1931 was implemented during the Hoover Administration. This act raised the tariff on thousands of goods imported into the United States. It was designed to increase the purchase of American made products by increasing the cost of imported goods. The farmers and the government benefited from the increased revenues. The Great Depression was a global recession, so other countries raised their respective tariffs on

American goods in retaliation, reducing international trade and slowing down global economic activities.

Andrew Mello, who was the Treasury Secretary during the Hoover Administration, implemented policies that involved cutting Income Taxes and reducing public spending, including excess profit taxes. Some even proclaimed that those policies favored the wealthy.
Andrew Mellon stated in an address in the administration prior to the election of Herbert Hoover:
> "A sound tax policy must take into consideration three factors. These factors must provide sufficient revenue for the government. The second factor to a sound tax policy is that it must lessen, so far as possible, the burden of taxation on those least able to bear it, and it must also remove the influences which might retard the continued steady development of business and industry on which so much of prosperity depends." (Joseph 2008)

The Roosevelt Administration

During the Roosevelt Administration, unemployment was at 24.99%, there were over 5,000 failed banks, and businesses and families had defaulted on their loans. Andre Mellon cut income taxes from 73% to 24%. The Revenue Act of 1932 increased taxes across the board at the end of Hoover's tenure. Franklin D. Roosevelt implemented the Reconstruction Finance Corporation. This policy was implemented a little too late to have an effect on the economy. The plan was intended to provide government-secured loans to financial institutions. FDR entered office in 1933 with the "First New Deal."

The First New Deal

The "First New Deal" included policies to pull America out of the Great Depression. The "First New Deal," also provided regulations for the protection of the financial institutions, investors, and beneficiaries, to prevent a tragic moment in world history from occurring again.

The Trading with the Enemy Act

The Trading with the Enemy Act gave the Treasury Secretary authority to confiscate the gold of private citizens and, in return, the citizens received an equivalent amount of paper currency. After 300 days since the passage of "Trading with the Enemy Act," most of the major and local banks, along with three quarters of Federal Reserve banks, which passed the federal inspection, were reopened to serve the public. Later, the Bank Act of 1933 was passed, and this legislation established Federal Deposit Insurance Corporation, which insured deposits up to $5,000.

Economy Act

Economy Act allowed the Federal government to purchase goods or services from other Federal government agencies. This act was designed to cut government employees' salaries and reduce pension paid to veterans by 15%, and cut government department budget by 25%. The ultimate goal of this bill was to balance the regular budget of the United State of America.

The Reagan Administration

During the Reagan Administration, the economy was in a deep recession and the inflation rate was at another all time high at 11.83%. The economy was suffering from high unemployment, about 3.5 points above the normal unemployment rate at 7.5%. Even though America was not at war during President Reagan's tenure, national defense expenditures increased about 40%.

Economic Recovery Act of 1981

Representative Jack Kemp and Senator William Roth wrote the Economic Recovery bill. This bill provided income tax rate cuts to stimulate economic growth by expense of depreciable property, providing business incentives for small businesses along with saving in financial institutions.

Tax Reform Act (TRA) of 1986

This bill was enacted to simplify the Internal Revenue Code. It also broadened its tax base and eliminated tax shelters and other preferences. Individual income tax rates were reduced at the top from 50% to 28%, while the bottom rates increased to 15% from 11%. In addition to the Tax Reform of 1986, capital gains were taxed at the same rate of ordinary income rates. Interest from consumer loans was no longer deductible. Finally, personal exemption and standard deduction were increased to provide the public with more tax relief.

Some of the incentives of the Tax Reform Act provided Home Mortgage Interest Deduction for those who owned homes. This was done to encourage those who rented to purchase homes. To provide home ownership incentives for the investment in housing units to those who do not have the resources to own a home, the Low Income Housing Credit was implemented. The Low Income Housing Credit provided a dollar for dollar deduction on taxable income to generate investment capital for multifamily housing units. The purpose was to provide housing to low income tenants under section 42 of the Internal Revenue Code.

TRA of 1986 increased the deductible contributed into an Individual Retirement Account to $2000. The Accelerated Cost Recovery System was used to determine the assets used in business for tax purposes. The Alternative

Minimum Tax was changed to expand the deduction, but the exemption amount was not adjusted for inflation.

The Tax Reform Act of 1986 gave a $25,000 net operating loss deduction to the less affluent landlords, whose Adjusted Gross Income was less than $100,000, and who did not physically live in the rental property for the greater of 14 days or 10% of rental days.

The focus of the economy in 1981 was the Economic Recovery Tax Act (ERTA). The Reagan tax cuts provided 25 percent "across the board" tax cuts in personal marginal tax rates. For the ERTA, reducing marginal tax rates and the economic incentives were intended to increase the flow of resources into production, boosting the economy and stimulating economic growth.

These policies were similar to the policies implemented in the past. The rich with high marginal tax brackets used the 1920's tax cuts of Andrew Mellon and the 1960's of President John F. Kennedy to reduce tax rates for everyone and increase tax payments. The Joint Economic Committee (JEC) released a report in 1996 on the results of the Reagan tax policies in comparison with Clinton policies. According to the JEC report, the policies that the Reagan Administration implemented favored the rich and wealthy. President Reagan lowered the tax rate, allowing the wealthy to keep more of business and personal income. Reagan also increased the national debt and put the proceeds in the pockets of the rich, while neglecting to spend the proceeds in programs such as health, education, or infrastructure projects.

The Clinton Administration

President Clinton planned a practice to jump-start the economy with a complex, interrelated combination of government programs and tax reform. Clinton also wanted to reduce the national debt by 50% in his four years.

Clinton implemented these government programs by increasing taxes for wealthy individuals and foreign corporations; and decreasing defense spending. To stimulate the economy, Clinton provided tax deductions and credits specifically targeted for domestic job creation. He strongly believed the federal government should invest in rebuilding the country's infrastructure (roads, bridges, and optical fiber cabling), and in retraining the country's workforce to effectively compete with German and Japanese workers. His goal was to increase the employment rate to increase economic growth.

Clinton's Tax Proposals

Clinton believed that:

1. The marginal income tax bracket should be raised from the current 31% to 36% on "wealthy" taxpayers, couples whose Adjusted Gross Incomes (AGI) exceed $200,000 and single taxpayers whose Adjusted Gross Incomes exceed $150,000;
2. "Middle class" taxpayers (couples earning $60,000 or less) may receive a tax-cut of $300 per dependent child; couples without dependents are slated to receive a $300 tax cut;
3. Taxpayers should be subject to a 10% surtax on incomes exceeding $1 million;
4. Corporations should not receive a tax deduction for payments to their chief executive officer greater than $1 million. Of these proposals, Congress will most likely pass the increase in tax rates on the wealthy and the tax-deduction limit on salaries paid to corporate CEO's. Whether the other proposals will pass is questionable; in recent speeches, Clinton's economic advisors have retreated from the middle-class tax cut proposal.

The George W. Bush Administration

George W. Bush, as the President, was very patriotic towards the United States of America. As the President, Bush did everything in his power to protect the citizens of America from terrorist attacks. In 2001, terrorists hijacked two planes and flew them into the World Trade Center in New York. President Bush felt the pain of the American people and vulnerability of the national security, so he invested America's resources into the War against Terror in Iraq and Afghanistan. Billions of dollars were spent in foreign policy. Additionally, in 2001 Bush implemented the Economic Growth and Tax Relief Reconciliation Act of 2001.

Economic Growth and Tax Relief Reconciliation Act of 2001

This legislation cut the taxes of the American people for about $1.6 trillion dollars. This act also made some changes in the Internal Revenue Code. The changes to the Internal Revenue Code were made to the income tax rates, estate and gift tax, qualified and retirement plan rules. Changes made to the income tax rates were:

- New 10% bracket was created with single tax status be tax on income up to $6,000; Joint filing status income being taxed up to $12,000; Head of Household filing status income being taxed up to $10,000.

- The standard deduction was increased for joint filing status returns by doubling the standard deduction given to a single filing status return.
The Economic Growth and Tax Relief Reconciliation Act allowed first time participants in a 401(k) to rollover balances from non-qualified 401(a) Money Purchase Accounts, 403(b) Tax sheltered annuity, 457(b) governmental deferred compensation plans without any penalty. In addition, the catch up provision was added to help participants ages 50 or over to make additional contributions to their plans over the normal contribution limit.

The gift and estate taxes were also affected by the legislation the President signed into laws during 2001. One of the changes was that the top tax rate for gift tax was capped at 45%. It was proposed the $675,000 gift tax exclusion in 2000 would increase to $1,000,000 in 2002, then to $1,500,000 in 2004, $2,000,000 in 2006, and $3,500,000 in 2009. The legislation was repealed and the exemption remained at $1,000,000 in 2006, which also included the carryover basis provision that was added to allow donees to report more gains in the future transfers or exchanges.

Jobs and Growth Tax Relief Reconciliation Act of 2003

President Bush signed the Jobs and Growth Tax Relief Reconciliation Act of 2003 on May 28, 2003. The following is a brief summary of the more notable tax provisions. Many of the provisions in this new tax law were only temporary, applying to 2003 and 2004. After 2004, the provisions enacted in the Economic Growth and Tax Relief Reconciliation Act of 2001 will once again become effective.

Individual Provisions:
Child Tax Credit For 2003 and 2004, the child tax credit increases from $600 to $1,000. The $400 increase will be paid in advance starting in July for those who have filed a 2002 tax return. The advance will be calculated from information on the taxpayer's 2002 tax return. The amount of the 2003 child tax credit that taxpayers can claim in 2003 will be reduced by the advance payment.

In 2005, the child tax credit is scheduled to fall back to $700, but will gradually rise to $1,000 by 2010 under the Economic Growth and Tax Relief Reconciliation Act of 2001.

Marriage Penalty Relief For 2003 and 2004, the standard deduction for married couples will double to twice the amount of the standard deduction for single taxpayers. In 2005, the standard deduction for married taxpayers will fall to 174 percent of the standard for single taxpayers, and then gradually rises to double the amount by 2009.

For 2003, the standard deduction for single taxpayers remains at $4,750. The standard deduction for married taxpayers will rise to $9,500. Married taxpayers filing a separate return will claim the same standard deduction as a single person.

For 2003 and 2004, the 15 percent tax bracket will be twice that for joint filers as it is for single filers. After 2004, the 15 percent tax bracket falls to 180 percent of the maximum taxable income in the same bracket for unmarried individuals, as adjusted for inflation.

Tax Brackets Income levels for the 10 percent tax bracket is increased to $7,000 for single taxpayers and to $14,000 for joint filers for 2003. In 2004, these income levels will be indexed for inflation. This relief is temporary. The old thresholds of $6,000 and $12,000 will reappear in 2005. New tax rates, retroactive to January 1, 2003 are 10, 15, 25, 28, 33, and 35 percent for individuals.

Capital Gains Rates the maximum capital gain tax rate drops from 20 percent to 15 percent. The current 10 percent tax rate for lower income taxpayers dropped to 5 percent.

These new rates are effective for sales and exchanges taking place on or after May 6, 2003, and through December 31, 2007. The 15 percent rate continues in 2008.

The lower rates apply for both regular tax and alternative minimum tax purposes. In 2008, the 5 percent rate for lower income taxpayers drops to 0 percent, but only for 2008. On January 1, 2009, the 10 and 20 percent rates are reinstated.

The lower rates for property held five years or more is effectively repealed until 2009. These rates were 18 percent (8 percent for lower income taxpayers). The 8 percent rate is repealed effective May 6, 2003. Those taxpayers who would have qualified the 18 percent rate for sales in 2005-2008 receive no additional benefit other than the lower 15 percent rate.

NOTE: The maximum rate for long-term gains from the sale of some assets, such as collectibles, remains at 28 percent. In addition, unrecaptured Section 1250 gains remain unchanged at the maximum 25 percent.

Alternative Minimum Tax (AMT)

For 2003 and 2004, the AMT exemption amount is increased to $58,000 for married taxpayers and to $40,250 for unmarried taxpayers.

Business Provisions:

Section 179 Expensing For 2003, taxpayers can expense up to $100,000 in qualifying property. The phase-out threshold increases from $200,000 to $400,000. For 2004 and 2005, this amount will be indexed for inflation. The new law allows taxpayers to make or revoke a Section 179 expense election without first obtaining the consent of the IRS.

For 2003-2005, taxpayers can expense off-the-shelf computer software under Section 179.

Bonus Depreciation

The additional 30 percent bonus depreciation increases to 50 percent for qualifying property placed in service after May 5, 2003 and before January 1, 2005. The definition of qualifying property has not changed. Qualifying property must still be brand new property with a class life of 20 years or less. The new law increases the bonus depreciation amount that may be taken with respect to passenger automobiles from $4,600 to $7,650.

The 30 percent bonus depreciation continues to apply to property purchased between September 11, 2001, and May 6, 2003.

Corporate Estimated Tax Payments

The third quarter estimated tax payment for corporate taxpayers that is normally due on September 15, 2003, is not required to be paid until October 1, 2003.

Taxation of Dividends

Dividends received by an individual shareholder from a domestic or qualified foreign corporation will be taxed in the same manner as capital gain income. This translates to 15 percent for most Taxpayers and 5 percent for taxpayers at lower income levels.

Although this provision is retroactive to January 1, 2003, it is temporary, terminating on December 31, 2008. The 5 percent rate terminates on December 31, 2007 and falls to 0 percent for 2008.
This one-year break only applies to taxpayers in the 10 and 15 percent tax brackets.

Certain types of dividends are specifically excluded from the definition of "qualified dividend income" for purposes of the new law.

The exclusion applies to the following:

Dividends paid from a corporation exempt from tax under IRC Sections 501 and 521.

Amounts that would be deductible under IRC Section 591 (i.e., dividends paid on deposits in a mutual savings bank, credit union, savings and loan, etc.)

Any dividend described in IRC Section 404(k).

Dividends paid under IRC Section 246(c) that fail to meet the revised holding period; or the extent that the taxpayer is under payment obligations under IRC Section 246(c).

The new tax law also provides additional guidance with regard to dividend income. Dividends are to be treated as investment income (if the taxpayer elects) for purposes of IRC Section 163(d) (4) which limits the amount of the investment interest deduction. What this appears to means is that taxpayers will not be allowed both the benefit of the lower tax rates and the treatment of this dividend income as net investment income for purposes of deducting investment interest.

A "qualified foreign corporation" is an entity incorporated within a U.S. possession or is eligible for the benefits of a U.S. tax treaty. Dividends paid by a foreign corporation that are not qualified are eligible for the lower rates if the stock is traded on an established U.S. equities market. (NATP, www.natptax.com/taxact2003.pdf)

The Obama Administration

President Obama's Economic Stimulus Plan

Today in America, as we know, Barack Obama has made history by being the first African-American President in the United States. History is taking place in a time that we as a nation must hold strong, in order to make it through the hard times we are currently facing as a whole. The U.S. is in a bad position, experiencing a recession that has placed our economy in bad shape; but it is still not as bad as The Great Depression. We have had back-to-back quarters of negative GDP growth, unemployment has risen from 5.2% to 7.8%, and banks have been tight on lending money due to the fear that consumers will stop paying because of financial difficulties. Banks have also cut credit limits and raised interest rates. Consumption and investment remain low due to inflation; there is a decrease in consumer spending and a nominal money supply, making the output of money lower, contributing to the recession.

Along with the recession, we are also in a current national debt in excess of ten trillion dollars ($10,731,057,110,570.31). The cause of this is that as a country, we are spending more than we make. As individuals, we take out loans simply because it easier than actually accumulating the money ourselves, even though we do not have the money to pay the lenders back. Businesses are also spending more money than they are making due to low levels of consumption, and this has caused many businesses to file for bankruptcy and go under. Everyone seems to be taking out loans and having trouble paying them back. This causes a domino effect, as the banks are affected negatively as well because they are lending too much money and not receiving enough of it back. Therefore, the banks are now stricter when it comes to lending money, and as a result, they are unable to help out the businesses. That is when the government has to step in and help out the businesses by bailing them out.

However there is also a problem when it comes to the government, because they are spending more money than they are receiving (Government Spending> Tax Revenue). This means that the money we have in our possession right now is owed to other countries, because none of it is really ours. We borrow from other countries, and eventually if these countries see that we are having trouble making payments and pulling ourselves out of debt, they will stop lending us money. Eventually, we would have no money to lend anyone, or to help our businesses, making unemployment skyrocket, because of the lack of money, making levels of consumption sink even lower. This would be a disaster!

Our President, Barack Obama, has been quick to make positive changes in our current economic crisis, putting forth plans for an $810 Billion Economic Stimulus Bill that will help to better our economy. Along with that, there is a plan for $300 Billion worth of tax cuts to help increase consumer spending, and lower long term government spending. However, there have been numerous arguments between the Democratic and Republican parties, because of their differing outlooks. The Republican Party's approach is that there is no need for such a stimulus package, and subsequently they voted against passing the bill. No Republican approved of the Stimulus package. They feel that the legislation has too much spending and not enough tax cuts. They believe in a hands-off approach in regards to the economy, which is a classical approach. This means letting the market heal itself.

Democrats, on the other hand, are in favor of the Keynesian approach, which involves the government helping to fine-tune the economy. The fiscal stimulus plan will help the weak economy to increase its activities, by increasing aggregate demand in the short run. In addition, along with the Bill, the tax cuts will discourage aggregate demand from falling. If the plan works, there will be no need for businesses to lay off workers. In my opinion, the Keynesian approach is a great idea, because of the government involvement in helping us to recover from this economic crisis. The plan requires much from the government, and though the idea of their involvement is good, in my opinion, the plan must be well thought out, and executed wisely. I am confident that President Barack Obama and his team are capable of following through on the plans that they have set forth to accomplish. I disagree with the Republican approach, which tends to be more conservative, like the classical "hands-off" policy mentioned earlier. They believe that the stimulus bill would be a waste, and lead us even further into the downward spiral that has already beset our economy. This would not be in the best interest of anybody involved. I am eager to see positive results for the short and long term.

There are arguments as to how to go about this economic crisis, as a nation. There are two policies of how the government or the Federal Reserve should go about this situation. Monetary policy is under the control of the Federal

Reserve, and it has the power to change interest rates and money supply to expand or contract aggregate demand. During a recession, the Federal Reserve usually lowers its interest rate and increases the money supply. In the fiscal policy, during a recession, the government would give tax cuts and usually increase government spending. However, since we are both in a recession and in a pretty deep national deficit, the government should go forth and use the fiscal policy. The government should also lower its spending along with the rest of the nation, because of the twin blows of the recession and debt, along with tax cuts, which like I mentioned earlier, would help aggregate demand from lowering. We should only purchase the goods, services and resources that are needed and start saving. We cannot forget that a big part of our problem is due to the fact that people purchased things that they did not need with loans and credits cards, without being sure that they would be able to pay them back.

In conclusion, the position of our economy is not a secret. Barack Obama's economic stimulus plan is not perfect, but it is still a great plan. Republicans and other groups want to do nothing about our current situation; they want to let the markets "heal" themselves, and once again believe that this stimulus bill would be a waste of money. Our President said that he refuses to do nothing, and with an economic time like this, he is going to take action. If nothing were done to help aid our economy, we would be in serious trouble. I believe that our government is taking the right steps to aid in the recovery of the United States of America.

The Economy through the Decades

America experienced more economic growth than any other country during the 20th century. The Great Depression caused by the Stock Market Crash of 1929 and turned America's focus to more regulations to preserve the traditions of individualism and prosperity. The country and the economy were back to their paths, and carrying on the traditions of individualism and prosperity, along with growth after the proactive response of President Franklin D. Roosevelt from the crisis.

1950 - The decade of postwar reconstruction began with unparalleled growth in the public sector and the welfare state. There was corresponding growth in total tax revenue, especially in the rate of social security contribution for financing the welfare state.

1960 - Economic growth and low unemployment fiscal policy was dominated by a new view that the government's fiscal policy's main function was to act as an instrument to regulate aggregate demand. Optimum trade off between inflation and unemployment is lowering tax and increasing government spending.

1970- Transition from high growth to stagflation oil shock, little worry was felt at the collapse of the fixed exchange rate or the commodity and food price boom. New tax handles, value added tax and spread withheld income tax. Global deterioration remained after the decline of total tax revenue and personal income tax.

1980- Further decline in macroeconomic performance with high unemployment levels. Tax distorts and low taxes were used to achieve micro-economic objectives. Lowering income tax, broadening of the income tax base, and flatting the personal income tax were some of the policies enacted to stimulate the economy and increase total tax revenue.

1990 - The economy continued to decline especially in 1993. The national budget was at the levels of 1983. The deficit reduction became the main priority of the government. Increase in total tax revenue, a reduction in the growth of government expenditures, and privatization in the country was in a surplus, government having an active approach to keep the economy stable by using policies of the past from the 1960's.

The National Debt

The national debt has never decreased since the Andrew Jackson Administration that brought the national debt below twenty thousand dollars. After the Jackson Administration, the national debt has increased and we have never been able to balance the budget. During both World Wars, the national debt increased. The debt continued to grow decades after, until President Clinton entered the White House. At that time, President Clinton did balance the budget, and reduced the national debt. The national debt was reduced during the Clinton Administration, however, the Bush Administration changed the balanced budget into more of a national deficit. The Bush Administration spent more money on the war in the twenty-first century, an investigation for the weapons of mass destruction, the search for Osama Bin Laden, and continued to borrow debt on top of debt. Most of the funds spent were concentrated on the military and foreign projects; however, our domestic issues were not given any thought. The water levies in New Orleans needed attention before being destroyed by Hurricane Katrina. The outdated bridge that collapsed in Minnesota, schools in our nation that are in need of dire repair, including the education system, and a broken down medical care system that charges high prices for premiums but provides minimum service for patients. The attitude of the Bush Administration is similar to the Reagan Administration, but with a twist.

In an article written by Steve McGourty, he gives an analysis of the U. S. National Debt over the century. I found the information very enlightening and informative. In the article, Steve McGourty writes.

> Our nation began its existence in debt from the Revolutionary War. Jefferson argued to eliminate the debt, and Hamilton argued it was necessary to keep the nation together. The Hamiltonians won, the conservatives of their time, and consequently it has been argued that this difference between these two founders was the beginning of the liberal/conservative split in our country.

FIGURE 1

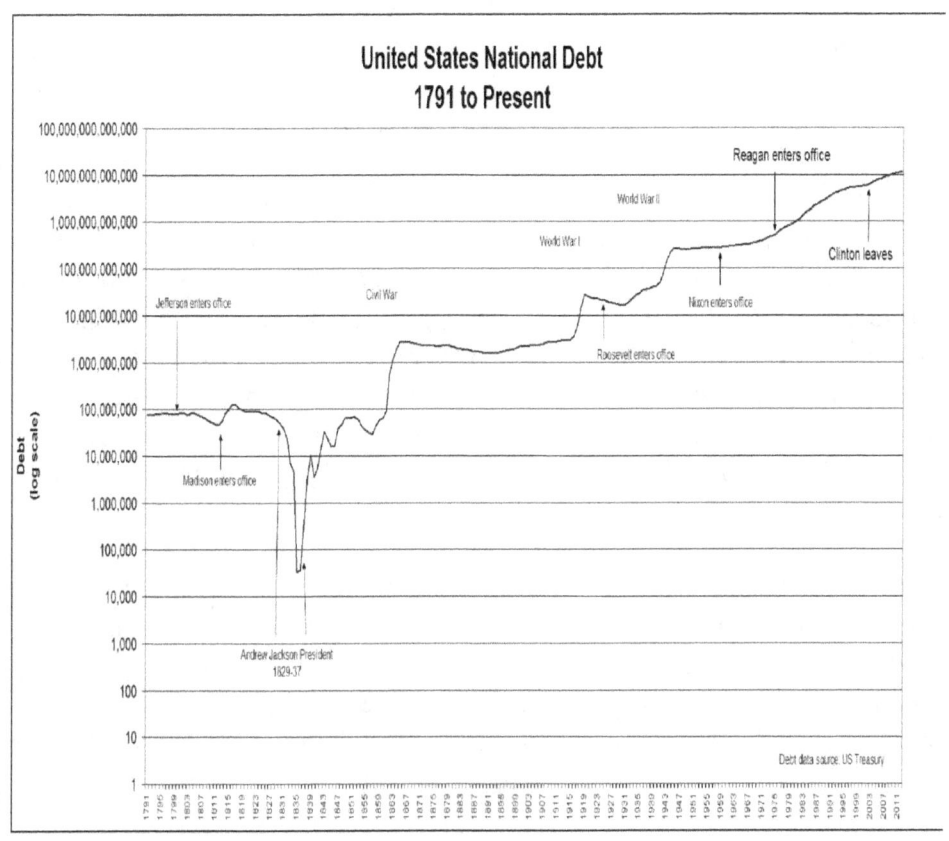

Figure 1 shows that we keep that original debt until the Jackson administration. Jackson did not believe in debt, or banks for that matter, and he made a real effort to eliminate all federal debt. He got it down to $18,000 just before leaving office. As you can see, there has not been another serious attempt to reduce the debt significantly since then. It is clear that debt increases from every major war, and it is equally clear to see that the debt is hardly ever reduced. Even when it is reduced, it is not by much, or for very long. This obvious fact seems to be overlooked by the folks that tell us they want to reduce your taxes and shrink government – every time they increase the debt it is forever, because this nation does not pay its debt off, ever!

Since 1938, the Democrats have held the White house for 35 years, the

Republicans for 36. Over that time, the national debt has increased at an average annual rate of 8.5%. In years, Democrats were in the White House there was an average increase of 8.3%. In years, the Republicans ran the White House the debt increased an average 9.2% per year. Those averages are not that far apart, but they do show a bias toward more borrowing by Republicans than Democrats even including World War II.

If you look at the 60+ year record of debt since the end of WWII, starting with Truman's term, the difference between the two parties' contributions to our national debt level change considerably. Since 1946, Democratic presidents increased the national debt an average of only 3.2% per year. The Republican presidents stay at an average increase of 9.2% per year. Republican Presidents out borrowed and spent Democratic presidents by a three to one ratio. Putting that in very real terms; for every dollar a Democratic president has raised the national debt in the past 63 years Republican presidents have raised the debt by $2.84[5].

Prior to the Neo-Conservative takeover of the Republican Party there was not much difference between the two parties' debt philosophy. They both worked together to minimize it. However, the debt has been on a steady incline ever since the Reagan presidency. The only exception to the steep increase over the last 30 years was during the Clinton presidency, when he brought spending under control and the debt growth down to almost zero.

Comparing the borrowing habits of the two parties since 1981, when the Neo-Conservative movement really took hold and government spending raced out of control, it is extremely obvious that the big spenders in Washington are Republicans and their party's presidents. The only Democratic president since then, Mr. Clinton raised the national debt an average of 4.3% per year. The Republican presidents (Reagan, Bush, and Bush II) raised the debt an average of 10.8% per year. That is, for every dollar a Democratic President has raised the national debt in the past 30 years, Republican presidents have raised the debt by $2.52[6]. Any way you look at it, Neo-Conservative Republican presidents cannot or will not control government spending.

For the first eighteen years after WWII, Truman (1945-53), Eisenhower (1953-61) and Kennedy (1961-63) all worked vigorously to keep spending under control. Of the seven years Truman was in office, the national debt came down in four. In 1946 & 7, with a Republican Congress for his first two years in office he brought down spending. The following year, with a Democratic Congress he reduced what was commonly called the "War Debt" again. Two of the eight years Eisenhower served as President saw debt reduction during the years when Democrats were in charge of Congress, 1956 & 7. Kennedy reduced the debt by over 4% his first year in office, 1961, then it went up slightly his next two years. JFK was dealing with a democratically controlled House and Senate when he managed to reduce the debt.

Since 1961, the United States national debt has never gone down.

It is interesting to note who controlled Congress versus what party was in the presidency during the seven years that the debt was reduced throughout the terms of Truman, Eisenhower and Kennedy. Three times the Democratic Party controlled both Houses of Congress and the Presidency (1948, 1951 & 1961). The other four years all had a mix of control, with Republicans in the White House (1956 & 1957), in charge of Congress (1946 & 1947), but never both. At no time since 1945 when Republicans have been in total charge of both elected branches of government have they ever reduced spending. They talk about it a lot, but they never deliver.

While the debt did go up every year during Johnson's time in office (1963-69), he was the last President before Clinton to submit a balanced budget, and Johnson did this during a time of a very hot Cold War. Johnson's average was a debt increase of 3% for the six years he served. He had a Democratic Congress to work with all his years in office.

Even Nixon (President from 1969 to 1974, when he resigned in disgrace) only had one year when he raised the debt more than 6%, 1971. His average was 5% for the six years he was in office. Between uncontrolled inflation and Ford's conservative bend the debt increased 17% his first full year in office (1975), and 13% his second (1976). Ford's plan to impose a policy of price controls failed to bring government overspending and inflation under control. Both these Presidents faced an opposition Congress controlled by Democrats during their time in office.

Starting in 1977, President Carter tried to control government spending even during inflationary times. The national debt increased an average of 9% per year while he was in office, and his policies eventually brought inflation under control with the help of a semi-cooperative Democratic Congress. He was thrown out of office after one term for making and implementing the hard decisions required to cut spending and deal with the energy crisis. (Had we followed his policies all these years we would not be dependant on foreign oil as we are now under Republican leadership.)

As President Reagan entered office in 1981, he repeatedly called for a balanced budget amendment to the Constitution, yet never submitted a balanced budget himself[7]. Many on the right reflexively blame the democratically controlled Congress for the "big spending" during his administration, even though Republicans controlled the Senate for the first six years of his two terms. Only during the last two years of the Reagan administration was the Congress completely controlled by Democrats, and the records show that the growth of the debt slowed during this period. It appears that the frequently referenced Reagan's Conservative mythology is contrary to the truth, he was an award winning, record setting liberal spender and government grower.

The fact is that Reagan was able to push his tax cuts through both Houses of Congress, but he never pushed through any reduced spending programs. His weak leadership in this area makes him directly responsible for the unprecedented rise in borrowing during his time in office, an average of 13.8% per year. The increase in total debt during Reagan's two terms was larger than all the debt accumulated by all the presidents before him combined. From 1983 through 1985, with a Republican Senate, the debt was increasing at over 17% per year.

While Mr. Reagan was in office this nation's debt went from just under 1 trillion dollars to over 2.6 trillion dollars, a 200% increase. The sad part about this increase is that it was not to educate our children, to improve our infrastructure, to help the poor, or even to finance a war. Reagan's enormous increase in the national debt was not to pay for any noble cause at all; his primary unapologetic goal was to pad the pockets of the rich. The huge national debt we have today is a living legacy to his failed Neo-Conservative economic policies. Reagan's legacy is a heavy financial weight that continues to apply an unrelenting drag on this nation's economic resources.

George Bush Sr. meekly followed in Reagan's shadow after his election in 1988, by increasing the debt on average a mere 11.8% a year during his four years as President. In his last year in office, he quite responsibly worked with Democrats to raise taxes to help reduce the massive yearly increases in the national debt.

This bipartisan plan got the growth down to under 11% in 1992, but it was too little too late and did not make much difference in the overall trend. The Neo-Conservatives controlling the Republican Party rewarded him for putting the nation's future above his party's ideology by throwing him out of office even though it had hardly been a year since he was credited with winning the Gulf War.

In 1993, President Clinton inherited the deficit spending problem and did more than just talk about it; he fixed it. In his first two years, with a cooperative Democratic Congress, he set the course for the best economy this country has ever experienced. Then he worked with what could be characterized as the most hostile Congress in history, led by Republicans for the last six years of his administration.

Yet, under constant personal attacks from the right, he still managed to get the growth of the debt down to 0.32% (one third of one percent) his last year in office. Had his policies been followed for one more year the debt would have been reduced for the first time since the Kennedy administration? Contrary to the myth fostered by our right-wing friends, under a Democrat, revenue increased and spending decreased.

When President Bush II came into office in 2001, he quickly turned all that progress around. With the help of a Republican controlled Congress he immediately gave a massive tax cut based on a failed economic policy; perhaps an economic fantasy describes it better. The last year Mr. Clinton was in office the nation borrowed 18 billion dollars. The first year Mr. Bush II was in office he had to borrow 133 billion[8].

The first tax cut Bush pushed through a willing Republican Congress caused an upswing in government borrowing that was supposed to stimulate the economy, but two years later Bush had to push through yet another tax cut. The second tax cut was needed because it was clear that the first one did not work. Economic history tells us the second did not work either. Because of his entire tax cutting with no cutting in spending, in 2003 President Bush set a record for the biggest single yearly dollar increase in debt in the nation's history. He did it again in 2004, increasing the debt more than half a trillion dollars.

Since 2003, total borrowing has typically been around $500,000,000,000 per year. Even Mr. Reagan never increased the debt that much in a single year; Mr. Reagan's biggest increase was only 282 billion, half of GWB is outrageous spending. Because of the fact that the debt was already pretty high when Bush II entered office, his annual rate of increase is only averaging 7% per year so far.

In 2006, he was holding press conferences bragging that the debt was increasing at the rate of only 300 billion dollars a year, yet in reality it was twice that. Again, the facts do not match Neo-Con rhetoric.

Of course, 7% growth is a misleading figure, as it does not make clear that by so drastically increasing the total debt, the amount of the annual US budget dedicated to service the debt has grown to almost 10%. Thanks to misguided Neo-Con ideological thinking, over a tenth of our budget does nothing to contribute to the growth or health of the nation. If interest rates go up our country will be in real trouble.

It does not matter if you call it a war or an occupation, supporting Iraq is expensive. It just boggles the imagination of any fiscally responsible person that the Republican Congress and President have repeatedly cut taxes during this overly aggressive and very expensive era for our military. The nation is borrowing money so that we can spend more on our military than all the other nations on Earth combined, and still the Neo-Cons are calling for even more tax cuts and even more military spending.

Mr. Bush is constantly claiming that the economy is great! What he leaves out is that he is buying that simulated good economy with his borrowed dollars; it is a false economy that is starting to crash. Recent bank and insurance company failures are proving that this federal borrowing can not go on forever, but what is the answer we are being given to this problem – borrow more money to cover the bad debt already out there! If a Democrat was suggesting this course of action, you can bet a bevy of Republicans would be screaming in unison that Congress is Socializing Wall Street. (McGourty, 2008)

Conclusion

Throughout the time of America's history, Americans have enjoyed a great deal of prosperity. During the 1950's, America has been the only country to develop the fastest economy after suffering from a few economic meltdowns and cultural rivalries. The only issue in America's history that is not the best representation of the country is its debt finance situation.

For example, the only time in American history that an administration brought down the national debt was in the 17th century. During the 17th century, Andrew Jackson was the only President in American history to minimize the national debt. His conviction of "not spending more that what you have" allowed his administration to just simply balance the budget and reduce the debt balance. Since then, the national debt has tripled and quadrupled. Abraham Lincoln raised the taxes to finance the Civil War. The American people during that time invested in an unnecessary war.

After the Civil War was over the national debt would never be brought back down to the $10,000 balance of the Jackson Administration. In the Spanish-American War, the President used estate taxes to finance that war. The President introduced the estate tax as the new base as a source of governmental revenues. Again, the taxes were increased during World War I under the Woodrow Wilson Administration.

After World War I was over, the Presidents who did not have faith in big business were replaced. The Republican Presidents entered office with the intention to have little government and reduced taxes that benefited the wealthy and powerful. The government got involved with private affairs by letting businesses monopolize and reduce competition.

President Hoover, along with the help of Andrew Mellon, Treasury Secretary, implemented tax policies that gave across the board tax cut to all citizens. However, these tax cuts benefited the wealthy and their agendas. That soon ended during the 1930's during the Stock Market Crash and the Banking Meltdown, which caused the country to lose a substantial amount of general revenues.

Soon after the Roosevelt Administration was out of office, America was faced with another world war. World War II caused the national debt to increase, leading to the American people having higher taxes. The increase in tax was earmarked for the funding of the world war.

However, when the war was over, the country was faced with high unemployment and inflation. The remedy to this symptom was reducing taxes to give the citizens more disposable income and influence spending to perpetuate more economic growth. The tax reduction occurred throughout the 1960's - 1980's.

Ronald Reagan continued to lower taxes and he made changes to the Internal Revenue Codes, for example allowing more depreciation to be deducted on business income.

The tax reduction continued in the 1990's, however, federal spending was reduced during the Clinton Administration.

The Clinton Administration left office with national surplus. When George W. Bush took office, the national budget was at a surplus. Then his administration started creating deficit spending; in addition, taxes were reduced, capital gains were reduced, exemptions were increased, and new tax bases was created.

Based on this research, I conclude that the tax policy trend is that when the country is doing fine, meaning employment is great and inflation is controlled, taxes will be lower and government spending will increase. When the country is in the red, the government will spend more to bail out the most vital industries, taxes will be raised to fund those vital industries, and provide jobs to unemployed.

However, a new trend will emerge, because the policies of the past are designed for manufacturing and closed economy. Currently, the global economy is causing changes to our fiscal policies of the past. The new powers are emerging like China, and that country is growing at an increasing rate and their influence on technology is having an effect our domestic business and fiscal policies.

Presidents in the 20th and 21st Century

Theodore Roosevelt	1901 – 1909
William H. Taft	1909 – 1913
Woodrow Wilson	1913 – 1921
Warren G. Harding	1921 – 1923
Calvin Coolidge	1923 - 1929
Herbert Hoover	1929 – 1933
Franklin D. Roosevelt	1933 – 1945
Harry S. Truman	1945 – 1953
Dwight D. Eisenhower	1953 – 1961
John F. Kennedy	1961 – 1963
Lyndon B. Johnson	1963 – 1969
Richard M. Nixon	1969 – 1974
Gerald Ford	1974 – 1977
Jimmy Carter	1977 – 1981
Ronald Regan	1981 – 1989
George W. H. Bush	1989 – 1993
William J. Clinton	1993 – 2001
George W. Bush	2001 – 2009
Barack H. Obama	2009 – Present

Treasury Secretaries of the 20th and 21st Century

Lyman J. Gage	3/6/1897 – 1/31/1902
Leslie M. Shaw	2/1/1902 – 3/3/1907
George B. Cortelyou	3/4/1907 – 3.7/1909
Franklin MacVeagh	3/8/1909 – 3/5/1913
William G. McAdoo	3/6/1913 – 12/15/1918
Carter Glass	12/18/1918 – 2/1/1920
David F. Houston	2/2/1920 – 3/3/1921
Andrew Mellon	3/4/1921 – 2/12/1932
Ogden L. Mills	2/13/1932 – 3/3/1933
William H. Woodin	3/4/1933 – 12/31/1933
Henry Morgenthau, Jr	1/1/1934 – 7/22/1945
Fred M. Vinson	7/23/1945 – 6/23/1946
John W. Snyder	6/25/1946 – 1/20/1953
George M. Humphrey	1/21/1953 – 7/29/1957
Robert B. Anderson	7/29/1957 – 1/20/1961
C. Douglas Dilon	1/21/1961 – 4/1/1965
Henry H. Fowler	4/1/1965 – 12/20/1968
Joseph W. Barr	12/21/1968 – 1/20/1969
David M. Kennedy	1/22/1969 – 2/11/1971
John B. Connally	2/11/1971 – 6/12/1972
William E. Simon	5/8/1974 – 1/20/1977
W. Michael Blumenthal	1/23/1977 – 8/4/1979
Donald T. Regan	1/22/1981 – 2/2/1985
James A. Baker, III	2/3/1985 – 8/17/1988
Nicholas F. Brady	9/16/1988 – 1/17/1993
Lloyd M Bentsen	1/10/1995 – 7/2/1999
Lawrence H. Summers	7/2/1999 – 1/20/2001
Paul H. O'Neill	1/30/2001 – 12/30/2002
John W. Snow	2/3/2003 – 6/29/2006
Henry M. Paulson, Jr	7/10/2006 – 1/20/2009
Timothy F. Geithner	1/26/2009 - Present

Bibliography

AICPA. <u>Guiding Principles of Good Tax Policy A Framework for Evaluating Tax Proposals.</u> (2001). Retrieved February 25, 2009. www.aicpa.org

Chambers, John Whiteclay. <u>Tyranny of Change.</u> (2000). Rutgers University Press. Pg. 187-188

Greenberg, David. <u>Calvin Coolidge.</u> (2007). Macmillian. Pg. 71-74

<u>Herbert Hoover.</u> (2009). www.spartacus.schoolnet.co.uk/usahoover.htm. Retrieved February 17, 2009

Ippolito, Dennis S. <u>Why Budgets Matter: Budget Policy and American Politics.</u> (2004) Penn State Press. 2004. Pg. 344

Joint Economic Committee. <u>The Reagan Tax Cuts: Lessons for Tax Reform.</u> (1996) Retrieved March 11, 2009. From www.house.gov/jec/welcome.htm

Joseph, J. <u>Tax History Project: Tax Cuts, Confidence, and Presidential Leadership.</u> (2008) Retrieved February 17, 2009, from Tax Analysis: http://www.taxhistory.org/thp/reading.nsf

Keynes, John Maynard, <u>The General Theory of Employment, Interest, and Money.</u> (1936). New York: Harcourt Brace.

Lenter, David; Slemrod, Joel; Shackelfor, Douglas. <u>Public Disclosure of Corporate Tax Return Information: Accounting, Economics and Legal Perspectives.</u> (2003). National Tax Journal. Dec 2003 Forum on Public Disclosure of Corporate Tax Returns.

McGourty, Steve. <u>United States National Debt: An Analysis of the President Who Are Responsible For the Borrowing.</u> (2005).

McNamee, Stephen J, Miller, Robert K. <u>Inheritance and Wealth in America.</u> (1998) Second Edition, Springer Publishing.

National Association of Tax Professionals. <u>Jobs and Growth Tax Relief Reconciliation wAct of 2003 (H.R. 2).</u> Retrieved April 16, 2009. From http://www.natptax.com/taxact2003.pdf

President William H. Taft's Message to Congress. (1909). The Congressional Records. Pg. 3344

Stein, Herbert. (1996). Why JFK Cuts Taxes. Retrieved February 23, 2009 The Wall Street Journal. From http://www.msjc.edu/econ/jfk022502.htm

The Budget and Economic Outlook: Fiscal Years 2004-2013, Appendix A, The Expiration of Budget Enforcement Procedure Issue and Options.
http://www.cbo.gov/ftpdoe.cfm?index=4032&type=08sequence-7

Woodrow Wilson (856-1924) Domestic Affairs.
American President Online Reference Source. Retrieved February 27, 2009
http://millercenter.org/acedemic/americanpresident/wilson/essay/biology/4